Jesse Tree Devotions

A Family Activity for Advent

by Marilyn S. Breckenridge

Augsburg Fortress

PREFACE TO PARENTS

This booklet is written and designed to help families prepare for Christmas and the celebration of Christ's birth. It traces the spiritual family tree of Jesus Christ in the tradition of the Jesse Tree, retelling many of the Bible stories that lead to Christ's birth.

The symbol of the Jesse Tree comes from Isaiah 11: "There shall come forth a shoot from the stump of Jesse, and a branch shall grow out of his roots." Jesse was the father of King David. When King Saul turned away from God, God rejected him as king and sent the prophet Samuel to the farm of Jesse near Bethlehem in search of a new king from among Jesse's eight sons. David, the youngest and a shepherd boy, was chosen. God told Samuel, "Arise, anoint him; for this is he" (1 Sam. 16:12). David became a great king and it was in his line, the Jesse line, that Jesus Christ was born a thousand years later in fulfillment of the prophecies.

To make a Jesse Tree, remove the foldout in the middle of this booklet and attach it to the refrigerator or a wall near the place where you will have your family devotions. Or, if you prefer, use a small artificial tree or select a shapely tree branch and set it in a pot in your home.

Each day during Advent, read together the Bible passage, the devotional thought, and the prayer for that day. Also, color and cut out the symbol at the bottom of the page, which represents the person or event for that day, and place it on the tree. On Christmas Day, place the symbol for Christ at the top of the tree.

To make this experience meaningful for children, involve them as much as possible. Young children, as well as older children, will enjoy coloring the symbols and placing them on the tree. This activity might take place either prior to or following the devotional reading— whatever works best in your situation. Young children, however, might appreciate the symbols more if they are completed following the explanations given in the readings. Upper elementary age children and older can locate and read the scripture passages and the daily devotionals. Take turns coloring the symbols and reading the scripture passages and the devotional thoughts.

Additional materials needed are:
- a Bible
- crayons or marking pens
- scissors
- tape or paste (or string, if you choose to use a real branch or tree.)

Jesse Tree Devotions
Illustrations by Avis Benson.
Copyright © 1985 Augsburg Fortress.
All rights reserved. Printed in the U.S.A.
ISBN 0-8066-2154-0, code 10-3475

The Jesse Tree

Pull out the Jesse Tree poster in the middle of the book. Hang the poster near the devotional meeting place. Or, acquire an artificial tree or tree branch to set up in the home.

READ ISAIAH 11:1-2.

Jesus was promised by God to his people long before he was born. In Isaiah we read that Jesus would be a "shoot" (like a new sprout that grows near lilac bushes or maple trees) from the family tree of Jesse. Now Jesse was the father of David, who became a great king of Israel. Jesus was born a thousand years after David as a shoot from the same family tree.

How far back can we trace our family tree? Families are important for many reasons. It is often because of our parents, grandparents, and great grandparents that we come to know and love Jesus Christ.

The symbols and daily thoughts for this first week in Advent will go even further back than David and his father, Jesse. They will go back to the very beginning of the world, to creation. That is when everyone's family tree began.

PRAYER

Thank you, God, for our family. Help us as a family this Advent season to prepare to celebrate Jesus' birthday at Christmas. As we think about his family tree, may we grow to love him more and to love our own family more. Amen

Cut out and color symbol 1, Stump of Jesse. Hang symbol on the Jesse Tree.

FIRST MONDAY IN ADVENT

Creation

Cut out and color symbol 2, Creation.

READ GENESIS 1:26-31.

From the very beginning people were special to God. They were different from the animals. They were created in God's image. That meant human beings were given special abilities and responsibilities. God told them to take care of the land, the animals, the birds, and everything that creeps upon the earth.

Do you have a pet? If so, are you taking good care of that pet? What can you do to take better care of your pet, the land, the animals, and the birds where you live?

PRAYER

Dear God, thank you for creating such a beautiful world and for all that is in it. Guide us as we do our part to care for your world and all your creatures. Amen

Hang Creation symbol on tree.

Cut out and color symbol 3, the Apple and Serpent.

READ GENESIS 3:1-7.

The story of sin's beginning and God's faithful love starts with the story of Adam and Eve. But both accounts continue throughout the Bible. Just as Adam and Eve sinned by disobeying God, so we sin. Sin is anything we think or do that separates us from God. Thus, the need for someone to come and save all people from their sins began long before the birth of Jesus Christ.

Let's think of the sins—the bad words, thoughts, and actions—that we have done recently. Then let's talk about them with each other. Remember, God sent Jesus to free us from our sins.

PRAYER

Thank you, God, for loving us so much that you sent Jesus to save us from our sins. Keep us strong when we are tempted to do wrong. Amen

Hang Apple and Serpent symbol on tree.

FIRST TUESDAY IN ADVENT

Adam and Eve

FIRST WEDNESDAY IN ADVENT

Noah

Cut out and color symbol 4, the Ark and Rainbow.

READ GENESIS 6:11-22; 9:8-13.

Noah is one of the fathers of the human race. In the story of Noah, we read that the world had become so sinful that God decided to destroy all the people living at that time. Only Noah and his family were saved. God told Noah to build a large boat, called an ark. It was 450 feet long, 75 feet wide, and had three decks. Noah and his family and two of every kind of animal lived on the ark during a flood that covered the earth.

After the flood God made a promise to Noah. He promised that he would never again destroy human beings and other living creatures of the world by a flood. We are reminded of this promise as Noah was, whenever we see a rainbow in the sky. It reminds us also that God loved his creation enough to give it a new start. We, too, are given a new start every time we turn to God.

PRAYER

Dear God, do not give up on us even when we forget you. Thank you for loving us enough to give us a new start every day. Amen

Hang Ark and Rainbow symbol on tree.

READ GENESIS 12:1-7 and HEBREWS 11:8.

The history of God's chosen people begins with Abraham and Sarah. In faith Abraham obeyed God's command to leave his home country. He left not knowing where he would go. But he believed God's promise to him of a land and a family that would grow into a great nation. Not only would Abraham and Sarah be blessed, but they would be a blessing to others.

As God promised his presence and guidance to Abraham and Sarah, so he promises it to us. Our family or a member of our family may be called to move or do something we or they have never done before. God promises to be with us as long as we are faithful to him.

PRAYER

O Lord God, help us to put our trust in you. May we go out in faith each day to serve you wherever we are called. Amen

Hang Tent and Camel symbol on tree.

FIRST THURSDAY IN ADVENT

Abraham and Sarah

FIRST FRIDAY IN ADVENT

Isaac

Cut out and color symbol 6, the Ram.

READ GENESIS 22:1-7.

When Abraham and Sarah were told they were going to have a son, they laughed. They thought they were too old to have children. When their son was born, they called him Isaac, which means "he laughed."

God promised that through Isaac a great nation would be born. But then God told Abraham to take his son and offer him as a sacrifice. Abraham loved God, but he also loved his son. Did Abraham love God enough to give up his son? Yes, Abraham trusted God. At the last moment, before Abraham could sacrifice his son, God provided a ram to be killed in Isaac's place.

Although Abraham did not have to give up his son, God did sacrifice his Son. Out of love for us, he gave up his Son, Jesus Christ.

PRAYER

Thank you, God, for loving us so much that you gave your only Son, Jesus Christ, to live and die for us. Amen

Hang Ram symbol on tree.

READ GENESIS 28:10-22.

Isaac's son Jacob had to leave his home because he had wronged his brother, Esau. Even so, Jacob discovered that God was with him and wanted to help him.

Today's reading from the Bible tells us about Jacob's dream. Dreams were a way God sometimes spoke to his people. In his dream, Jacob saw a ladder stretching from earth to heaven. God told Jacob that he would become the father of a great people. God kept his promise. From Jacob a great nation was born. From his 12 sons came the people of Israel, the family tree of Jesus Christ.

God speaks to us in various ways. Have any of us ever thought we heard God speaking in a dream? How does God usually speak to us today?

PRAYER

O Lord God, open our hearts and minds to you. We want to hear you when you speak to us. In our dreams, our thoughts, and our experiences guide us through the words of the Bible and through believing people. By your Spirit may we not only hear your Word but may we do it. Amen

Hang Ladder symbol on tree.

FIRST SATURDAY IN ADVENT

Jacob

SECOND SUNDAY IN ADVENT

God's People

Cut out and color symbol 8, the Star.

READ GENESIS 35:9-15.

From Jacob's 12 sons God formed a nation of people called Israel. The Old Testament is the story of these people. It tells of their successes as well as their failures. Sometimes they forgot God, but God never forgot them. God continued to raise up leaders to bring the people back to him. They looked for one last leader, the Messiah, to come to save them from their troubles forever.

This second week of Advent, we will read about some of the great leaders of Israel—Joseph, Moses, Ruth, Samuel, David, and Solomon. It is from David that the symbol of the star came to stand for the people of Israel. As we read about these biblical heroes, let us also think of some of our Christian leaders today. Who are some of today's Christian heroes?

PRAYER

O God, we thank you for those people who have been leaders in the faith through the centuries. We pray especially this day for those who lead us now in the faith. Help us to live as your people. Amen

Hang Star symbol on the tree.

Cut out and color symbol 9, the Coat of Many Colors.

READ GENESIS 37:1-4.

Joseph was the favorite son of Jacob. Jacob gave him presents that made Joseph's 11 brothers jealous. One time Jacob gave Joseph a coat of many colors. This coat and Joseph's dreams made his brothers angry. They decided to get rid of Joseph. They were going to kill him, but instead they sold him to some traveling merchants. The merchants sold Joseph as a slave in Egypt. In Egypt Joseph rose from slavery to become the man next in position and power to the pharaoh or king.

This story shows how God used the failures and wrongs of people for good. Through Joseph, God cared for his people. During a famine in the land of Israel, Jacob and his sons and their wives and children, 70 people in all, came to live in Egypt where Joseph had stored plenty of food. In Egypt the people of Israel lived for many years and became a great number.

Can we think of something that has happened in our life that seemed bad but then turned out for good? Maybe it was a move, a new school, or even an accident.

PRAYER

O God, help us to live together in peace. As we look for good in situations that seem hopeless, show us that you are working things out for our good. Amen

Hang Coat of Many Colors symbol on tree.

SECOND MONDAY IN ADVENT

Joseph

SECOND TUESDAY IN ADVENT

Moses

Cut out and color symbol 10, the Ten Commandments.

READ EXODUS 20:1-17.

After Joseph died, the people of Israel became slaves in Egypt. For many years they were slaves. Then God called Moses to lead his people out of Egypt and slavery. This great movement of the people of God out of Egypt and back to the Promised Land is called the Exodus. The Exodus is the greatest happening in the Old Testament. The people of God never forgot it. It was as important to Old Testament people as Jesus Christ is to the church and to us.

At Mount Sinai, in the desert on the way to the Promised Land, God gave Moses the Ten Commandments. These commandments were laws for the people to follow so that they would live in a way that pleased God.

Which of the commandments in Exodus 20 is the most important? Let's see Matthew 22:36-38 for Jesus' answer.

PRAYER

O Lord, we thank you for your commandments, which show us your will and also our need for Jesus Christ as our Savior. May we give him first place in our lives. Amen

Hang Ten Commandments symbol on tree.

Cut out and color symbol 11, the Sheaf of Grain.

READ RUTH 1:15-18.

Ruth was a woman from the land of Moab who married an Israelite. When her husband died, she remained faithful to his family and to their God. She returned with her mother-in-law, Naomi, to Naomi's old home in Bethlehem. There she gathered grain for herself and Naomi in the fields of a man named Boaz. Ruth later married Boaz. They became the parents of Obed, who was the father of Jesse and the grandfather of David. Thus, Ruth the foreigner became the great grandmother of David and an ancestor of Christ.

From this story we learn that no one is excluded from God's love. It also tells us that God sometimes uses people we wouldn't expect him to use to accomplish his purposes.

PRAYER

Dear Jesus, we thank you that you came to save all people. Move us to reach out in love to those people who are different from us. Amen

Hang Sheaf of Grain symbol on tree.

SECOND WEDNESDAY IN ADVENT

Ruth

SECOND THURSDAY IN ADVENT

Samuel

Cut out and color symbol 12, the Horn of Oil.

READ 1 SAMUEL 16:1-13.

Samuel was a prophet. A prophet is someone who speaks for God. Samuel was chosen by God to anoint the first two kings of Israel. Anointing is the pouring of oil on the head or breast of a person. It is a sign that God favors that person and wants to use him or her in a special way.

The first king that Samuel anointed was Saul. At first Saul was a good king. But then he became disobedient and refused to listen to Samuel's advice. God rejected him and told Samuel to anoint a new king. It was David, the youngest son of Jesse, whom Samuel anointed to be the new king of God's people.

In a way we are anointed at our Baptism, not with oil but with water. When water is poured on our head and a cross is made on our forehead or breast, it is a sign we are united with Jesus Christ and are now members of his church. God's power has touched us.

PRAYER

Thank you, God, for the gift of Baptism, which is a sign that we are your people. We seek to do your will at home, at school, and at work. Amen

Hang Horn of Oil symbol on tree.

14

Cut out and color symbol 13, the Crown.

READ 2 SAMUEL 5:1-5.

After Saul's death, David began serving as king. He ruled in Jerusalem for 33 years. During that time he became a great king. He was great because he trusted God and tried to obey God in everything he did as king. David made some mistakes, but he continued to turn to God for forgiveness and guidance. Israel became a strong nation under David's leadership.

Later, when the people of Israel looked for the Messiah, someone to save them, they looked for another king like David. They didn't get another king like David. Instead God sent Jesus Christ, who came from David's family line, the Jesse tree. Jesus is greater than any earthly king. He is the Savior of the whole world.

PRAYER

Dear God, we thank you for kings, presidents, and all the rulers of our world today. Make them great leaders who try to obey you.
Amen

Hang Crown symbol on tree.

SECOND SATURDAY IN ADVENT

Solomon

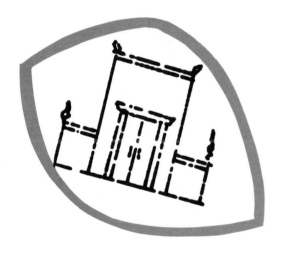

Cut out and color symbol 14, the Temple.

READ 1 KINGS 3:3-14.

Solomon followed his father, David, as king of Israel. He is remembered for his great wisdom and for the beautiful temple he built for God in Jerusalem. Some of his wise sayings are collected in the Old Testament book of Proverbs. The temple served the people of Israel as the central place of worship for over 350 years.

Worship continues to have a central place in the lives of God's people. Today we build churches as places to worship. In our church, we gather together as the people of God to gladly hear God's Word and to praise him.

PRAYER

Lord God, thank you for our church and for all the churches in the world. Help us to respect them as places where the Bible is taught and where you are worshiped. Amen

Hang Temple symbol on tree.

Prophecy

Cut out and color symbol 15, the Candle and Rose.

READ ISAIAH 42:5-9.

Throughout the history of God's people there have been prophets who told what was going to happen in the days to come. These prophets spoke God's word to his people. They directed the people in times of trouble; they scolded the people when they did wrong; and they continued to remind the people that they were God's chosen people.

The candle stands for the words the prophets spoke. It indicates the light of God. The rose stands for Christ. Christ was God's promises and the prophets' preaching come true.

During the days of this third week of Advent we will read some of the prophecies that spoke about Christ. The people had to wait a long time for these prophecies to come true. But as God promised, he did send the Messiah. He sent his very own Son, whose birthday we will be celebrating when Christmas finally comes.

PRAYER

Lord God, thank you for the prophets of old who preached your Word to the people of their day. We also thank you for our pastors and Christian teachers and all who help us to know you today. Amen

Hang Candle and Rose symbol on tree.

17

THIRD MONDAY IN ADVENT

Elijah

Cut out and color symbol 16, the Burning Altar.

READ 1 KINGS 18:17-24; 36-39.

The prophet Elijah lived 900 years before Jesus during a time of famine and drought in Israel. It did not rain and the crops did not grow. And the people of Israel were worshiping idols. But Elijah remembered God's promises and tried to tell the people about the one true God. To prove that only the Lord was God, Elijah entered into a contest with the priests of Baal, an idol. As we read in 1 Kings, God sent fire down to prove he was God. Then all the people shouted: "The Lord, he is God."

Sometimes we forget God. We stay home from church on Sundays to sleep in or to read the Sunday paper or to go hunting or fishing. When we do that, we grow away from God and begin to worship idols.

PRAYER

Loving God, forgive us for serving idols instead of you. Spark in us a desire to keep you first in our lives. Call us to be faithful in our worship of you. Amen

Hang Burning Altar symbol on tree.

Cut out and color symbol 17, the Hammer and Sword.

READ ISAIAH 2:4; 7:14; 9:6-7.

Isaiah was one of the greatest prophets of the Old Testament. He lived near the city of Jerusalem about 700 years before Christ. His prophecies brought hope to the people of Israel because he foresaw God's plan to save their nation. He said that people would one day make blades for their plows out of their swords, for there would be peace.

Isaiah also foretold the birth of a child who would be called Immanuel. Immanuel means "God with us." The child would be a new branch on the Jesse family tree. That child was Jesus Christ, whose birthday we are preparing to celebrate on Christmas.

PRAYER

May Isaiah's prophecies come true for us, O Lord. May the child he prophesied be received in our hearts this Christmas. Amen

Hang Hammer and Sword symbol on tree.

THIRD TUESDAY IN ADVENT

Isaiah

THIRD WEDNESDAY IN ADVENT

Jeremiah

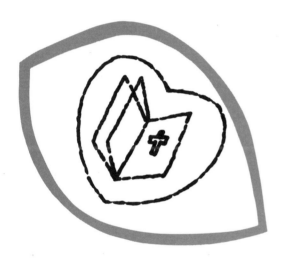

Cut out and color symbol 18, the Heart and Word.

READ JEREMIAH 23:5-6; 31:31-34.

The people of Israel again forgot God and lived wicked lives. This time God used the prophet Jeremiah to speak God's word to the people. But as Jeremiah had prophesied, the nations around Israel invaded and conquered them.

Still God looked after his people. He saved a few of them, and made a new promise to them. This new promise would come true when God raised up a new leader, a righteous Branch, to rule his people. That day came with the birth of Jesus Christ, 600 years later. Jesus established a new relationship with God's people based on love rather than on laws.

God wants us to love and obey him, not because he commands it but because we want to. That is the way we like things to be in our families also. We should do things for each other because we love each other, not because those things are demanded of us.

PRAYER

Lord God, we rejoice that you have not given up on your people. Thank you for the patience and love you continue to show us today in our lives. Strengthen us to do your will because we love you. Amen

Hang Heart and Word symbol on tree.

READ DANIEL 6:10-23.

In the year 598 B.C. King Nebuchadnezzar of Babylon conquered Jerusalem. Daniel was among the people of God who were captured and brought to Babylon. In Babylon, Daniel became a favorite of the king. As a result, some officials became jealous and tried to get rid of Daniel. They convinced the king to make a law that no one could pray to any idol or person, except to the king, for 30 days. Anyone found praying to someone else would be thrown into a den of lions.

As we read in the Bible story, Daniel continued to pray to God and so was thrown into the den of lions. What happened to Daniel?

No doubt, this story has been told many times to encourage the people of Israel to trust God even when their situation looked bad. Daniel shows that if God's people are faithful to God and never stop praying to him, they can overcome their enemies.

PRAYER

Dear Lord, we want to be faithful to you. Hold your promise before us so that we remember to say our prayers every day. Amen

Hang Lion symbol on tree.

THIRD THURSDAY IN ADVENT

Daniel

THIRD FRIDAY IN ADVENT

Nehemiah

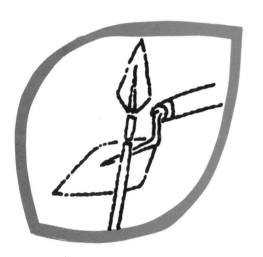

Cut out and color symbol 20, the Trowel and Spear.

READ NEHEMIAH 4:15-23.

Things looked hopeless for the people of God who were held captive in Babylon. Some settled easily into their new country, while others missed their homeland and longed to return to it. Again God remembered his people. As Isaiah had prophesied, King Cyrus of Persia conquered Babylon. The people of Israel were freed and allowed to return to Jerusalem, their ruined capital city.

Nehemiah directed the returning people to rebuild the walls of Jerusalem. Neighboring groups of people opposed the rebuilding, so the Jews worked holding their weapons in one hand in order to be ready to defend themselves. God was with them as he had promised. The walls were rebuilt and the people of Israel again lived in their homeland.

Sometimes we, too, must work under difficult conditions. Let's try to remember a time that we were able to do something that we thought would be impossible? As God was with Nehemiah and the people of Israel 450 years before Christ, so he is with us 1900 years after Christ.

PRAYER

Lord God, we look to you for courage and strength to meet every difficult time in our lives. Amen

Hang Trowel and Spear symbol on tree.

Cut out and color symbol 21, the Praying Hands.

READ LUKE 1:5-17.

Zechariah and Elizabeth had no children. One day when Zechariah, who was a priest, went into the Temple to burn incense, an angel appeared to him. And the angel said, "Do not be afraid, Zechariah, for your prayer is heard, and your wife, Elizabeth, will bear you a son, and you shall call his name John." Zechariah found the news too good to be true. Children were considered to be a great blessing. Would his prayer really be answered?

God promises to hear our prayers and to do those things that are good for us. An answer to prayer might be yes, no, or later. Think of something we have prayed for and have received. Also think of something we have prayed for and have not yet received.

PRAYER

Lord God, for the gift of children and the love of parents, we thank you. Make us a close, loving family. Amen

Hang Praying Hands symbol on tree.

THIRD SATURDAY IN ADVENT

Zechariah and Elizabeth

FOURTH SUNDAY IN ADVENT

Mary

Cut out and color symbol 22, the Lily.

READ LUKE 1:26-38.

It is almost Christmas. Soon we will celebrate the birth of Jesus Christ and the fulfillment of the Old Testament prophecies. These last few days before Christmas we will focus on events and people that are important in the Christmas story.

Today is a day to think of Mary, the mother of Jesus. When the time came for Jesus to be born, God's angel came to Mary. The angel said, "Do not be afraid, Mary, for you have pleased God. And he will cause you to have a baby son, and you shall call his name Jesus."

How surprising are God's ways! Through a poor, young woman from the town of Nazareth, God was going to come to his people. But God chose well. Mary responded in faith, saying, "Behold, I am the servant of the Lord; let it happen to me just as you have said."

PRAYER

O God, we thank you for Mary, the mother of Jesus, and for all loving mothers everywhere. Amen

Hang Lily symbol on tree.

(If today is Christmas Eve, skip to page 30.)

FOURTH MONDAY IN ADVENT

Joseph of Nazareth

Cut out and color symbol 23, the Carpenter's Tools.

READ MATTHEW 1:18-25.

Being Mary's husband brought its problems. Yet Joseph seemed to be the right man for Jesus' earthly father. Not much has been written about Joseph in the Bible. We know he was a descendent of David and that he worked as a carpenter. We also know that he was a good man.

In the story read today, Joseph showed his love for Mary as well as his faith in God. He did what the angel commanded. He stood by Mary, and when Jesus was born he acted as his father. Most likely, it was Joseph who gave Jesus his religious training. He also probably taught him carpentry skills. Because there is no mention of Joseph in later family accounts, it is believed that he died when he was still quite young.

PRAYER

Dear God, we thank you for Joseph and for all fathers who love and care for their families. Amen

Hang Carpenter's Tools symbol on tree.

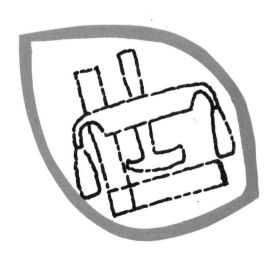

(If today is Christmas Eve, skip to page 30.)

FOURTH TUESDAY IN ADVENT

John the Baptist

Cut out and color symbol 24, the Shell.

READ MATTHEW 3:1-11.

About six months before Jesus was born, a son was born to Elizabeth and Zechariah. They named him John. Later he became known as John the Baptist. He was the last of the great prophets of Israel. He came to prepare the way for the Savior, Jesus Christ.

The shell is a symbol of Baptism that also stands for John the Baptist. John the Baptist preached that people should repent of their sins and be baptized. He baptized hundreds of people, including Jesus Christ. But his baptism was not exactly like ours today.

Let's talk about our family's baptisms. When were each of us baptized? Who were our sponsors? What does it mean to be baptized? For Christians, Baptism is God's way to give life in Jesus Christ and membership in his church.

PRAYER

Thank you, Lord, for the gift of Baptism. As we live each day as your children may we, like John the Baptist, prepare the way for Christ to come into the lives of others. Amen

Hang Shell symbol on tree.

(If today is Christmas Eve, skip to page 30.)

FOURTH WEDNESDAY IN ADVENT

Angel

Cut out and color symbol 24, the Angel.

READ HEBREWS 13:1-2.

Angels are spoken about in many of the stories of the Bible. They are messengers of God who usually bring good news. For example, it was an angel who told Mary that she had been chosen to be the mother of Jesus. It was also an angel who explained everything to Joseph. And it was an angel who brought the news of Jesus' birth to the shepherds.

When we think of an angel we picture a winged person who is both swift and beautiful. In real life, an angel could speak to us through our thoughts and our dreams, as well as in person.

In addition to being a messenger for God, an angel is one who watches over us. We pray to God, "Let thy holy angel have charge over us." That means we want to be protected and kept safe.

This Christmas you can be one of God's "angels." You can watch over someone and you can tell the good news that Jesus Christ is born.

PRAYER

God, make us your "angels" to others. Show us when to do good things for other people and how to tell everyone about the birth of Jesus your Son. Amen

Hang the Angel symbol on tree.

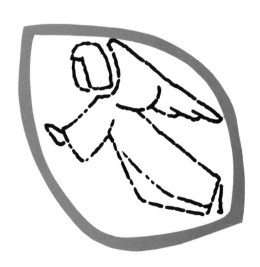

(If today is Christmas Eve, skip to page 30.)

FOURTH THURSDAY IN ADVENT

Shepherds

Cut out and color symbol 26, the Shepherd's Staff and Sandals.

READ PSALM 23.

Most of us have never seen a shepherd. But in the Bible we find many stories about shepherds. The Bible speaks of two kinds of shepherds—those who care for sheep and those who care for people. Both are pictured as being devoted to caring for their flocks. They lead them to green pastures and quiet waters. They find the lost and bring them home again.

It was to shepherds watching their flocks near Bethlehem that the angel appeared and announced the birth of Jesus. Later, Jesus spoke of himself as the Good Shepherd who was ready to die for his sheep. Yes, Jesus is the Good Shepherd. He was born, he lived, and he died for our good.

PRAYER

Dear Jesus, thank you for being our shepherd. Call us to follow you daily. Amen

Hang Shepherd's Staff and Sandals on tree.

(If today is Christmas Eve, skip to page 30.)

FOURTH FRIDAY IN ADVENT

Bethlehem

Cut out and color symbol 27, the Star of Bethlehem.

READ MATTHEW 2:1-6.

Sing "O Little Town of Bethlehem."

> O little town of Bethlehem,
> How still we see thee lie!
> Above thy deep and dreamless sleep
> The silent stars go by;
> Yet in thy dark streets shineth
> The everlasting light.
> The hopes and fears of all the years
> Are met in thee tonight.

Bethlehem was the birthplace of Jesus. The prophecy of Micah, which said that a ruler would come from Bethlehem, was fulfilled. Bethlehem was the setting for many important events in the Scriptures. It was the hometown of Jesus' family. Boaz and Ruth, their son Obed, his son Jesse, and Jesse's son David, all lived in Bethlehem. When a census was ordered, Mary and Joseph traveled to Bethlehem to be counted and taxed. There in a stable Mary gave birth to Jesus, because there was no room left for them in the inn.

The star is a symbol for Bethlehem because a special bright star shone over Bethlehem the night Jesus was born. It was also a special star that led the Wise Men to the newborn Christ.

PRAYER

> Dear Lord, open our hearts and minds to the message of the Christmas story. Jesus, enter our hearts and lives anew this Christmas. Amen

Hang Star of Bethlehem symbol on tree.

29

CHRISTMAS EVE

The Manger

Cut out and color symbol 28, the Manger.

READ LUKE 2:1-20.

Is there any story more beautiful than the Christmas story? In that manger lay the fulfillment of the prophecies—a shoot from the root of Jesse—and the greatest sign of God's great love for his people.

Sing "Away in a Manger."

> Away in a manger, no crib for his bed,
> The little Lord Jesus laid down his sweet
>   head;
> The stars in the sky looked down where
>   he lay,
> The little Lord Jesus asleep on the hay.

PRAYER

Dear Jesus, thank you for being born on that first Christmas. Be with us as we celebrate your birthday. As we open our gifts, we rejoice that you are the best gift of all. Amen

Hang Manger symbol on tree.

Cut out and color symbol 29, the Chi-Rho.

READ JOHN 1:1-18.

Sing "Joy to the World."

> Joy to the world, the Lord is come!
> Let earth receive its King;
> Let ev'ry heart prepare him room
> And heav'n and nature sing,
> And heav'n and nature sing,
> And heav'n, and heav'n and nature sing.

Today we celebrate the birth of Jesus Christ, who was born into the family tree of Jesse, the "son" of David, the child of Mary, the Son of God. Two Greek letters, *chi* and *rho* form a symbol for Jesus Christ. They remind us that it was not just an ordinary baby who was born in that stable years ago in Bethlehem. That child was God's Son. God became a human being, just like us. Let us worship him and keep him forever in our hearts.

PRAYER

> Lord God, we are filled with wonder and joy today because of your great love for us. Thank you for sending the Promised One, Jesus, to be our Lord and Savior. We praise his holy name. Amen

Place Chi-Rho symbol at the very top of the Jesse Tree.

CHRISTMAS DAY

Jesus Christ